M000160119

ABA Mini-Manual: Level One

Alan Schnee, Ph.D., BCBA-D

"Nature is not classical..." Richard Feynman

It's been almost 50 years since Ivar Lovaas first published, <u>The Autistic Child</u> (1977) and almost 40 years since the groundbreaking, "1987 study". Since then, the literature related to early intensive behavioral intervention has grown exponentially and broadcasts myriad viewpoints on implementation and guiding theory. However, it is not the purpose of this manual to weigh in on these views or approaches.

The ABA Mini-Manuals offer exercises across many core and advanced areas related to early intensive behavioral intervention. The highly detailed, step-by-step procedures offered in these manuals eliminates the guesswork on 'how to' set up, teach and develop many core and advanced abilities. As important, the ABA Mini-Manuals offer *a way to think about* constructing intervention. As such, the manuals illuminate, through countless examples, ways to link abilities, to integrate and interrelate them so that greater linguistic and behavioral complexity comes about.

Similarly, the ABA Mini-Manuals specify and enhance tool skills which underlie many abilities. Accordingly, sitting under basic matching abilities are scanning, short-term memory and shifting attention. These same abilities sit behind basic executive function tasks. Additionally, the manuals illustrate how certain capabilities can be leveraged in order to advance other abilities. For example, users of these manuals will see how matching can be employed as a vehicle to foster social awareness.

Finally, the ABA Mini-manuals emphasize the engineering aspects of intervention. Thus, building an intensive behavioral intervention program is to abide by the maxim, 'To intervene is to plan'; To know where one is headed, which constituent elements need to be in place, and how to relate them so that children may have their best chance to more fully join in our social practice. It is hoped that this effort will provide users with a sense, and firm foothold, for how to make this happen.

Table of Contents

Matching

For a brief discussion about matching and troubleshooting go to:

https://www.nexusais.com/mad-about-matching

	Basic Identity Matching
Purpose	<ul><li>To establish a basic routine of *receive, look, scan, and decide (making a comparison)*.</li><li>This routine targets fundamental perceptual and cognitive abilities including scanning, shifting attention between objects, and basic-level categorization.</li><li>Learn to compare and contrast</li></ul>
Set up	<ul><li>Place three distinct objects on the child's worktable. The objects should be separated by a few inches.</li></ul>
Procedure	1. Hand the child an object corresponding to one of the objects on the table and say: "Put with same" (or "match"). 2. When the child makes the match, remove the object and introduce another trial. 3. Use conventional discrete trial instruction.
Considerations	<ul><li>If the child has difficulty with this exercise, it is usually because they are not looking at the items they are holding or the objects on the table, or both. In other words, the child does not *compare* - they do not shift attention between the object in their possession and the objects on the table.</li><li>Strengthening attention to the object often requires ample practice (repetition), and use of a highly discrete routine.</li></ul>

	Instruction should be modified over time as children begin to shift attention flexibly to compare objects.
	• Increase the field size gradually (the number of objects on the table). This strengthens the child's scanning or searching ability and persistence. Eventually, the objects on the table should be presented in varied arrangements (linear, horizontally, random/disorganized).
	• Once the child can match identical objects, make the objects progressively more dissimilar (non-identical). This kind of basic-level categorization or 'stimulus generalization' requires considerable multiple exemplar teaching where the objects vary across many different kinds of details.
	• Once the child is able to match objects that are quite dissimilar, introduce identical *picture* matching. Follow the same procedure as object matching. Introduce non-identical pictures as the child makes progress. Once the child can match dissimilar pictures, start "Matching Object to Pictures".
Trouble-shooting	• Some children have difficulty with picture matching and special stimulus shaping procedures may be necessary. For instance, the pictures may be initially cut out to remove the background so they retain their idiosyncratic contours. • Sometimes children do not flexibly shift their attention between the stimuli in order to make the necessary comparisons. Target in target strategies may help, spreading items apart may help or sometimes elevating target items to a wall might encourage flexible shift of attention.
Permutations	• We like to build in 'problem solving' as early as possible. We will mount pictures on a wall that are out of reach. We then hand children matching pictures and ask them to "match". We provide chairs and step stools, which will allow the child to reach the target. This also encourages balance, greater

	fine motor control and scanning. Think of other variations.

	Matching Objects to Pictures
Purpose	• To further establish visual recognition of kinds and "unite" three-dimensional objects and their representations (two-dimensional objects).
Set up	• Place three distinct pictures on the worktable. The pictures should be separated by a few inches.
	• Use conventional discrete trial instruction.
Procedure	1. Hand the child a picture corresponding to one of the pictures on the table and say: "Put with same".
	2. When the child matches, remove the object and introduce another trial.
	3. Increase the field size gradually (the number of pictures on the table). This strengthens the child's scanning ability and persistence. Eventually, present pictures in varied arrangements (linear, horizontally, random/disorganized).
Considerations	• Once the child is proficient, make the objects and pictures increasingly more dissimilar.
	• Once the child is proficient with the previous step, reverse the arrangement; Present a picture and require the child to identify the corresponding object (see "Bring Same").

	Sorting (1)
Purpose	• To strengthen sustained attention to task (task completion).

6

	• Disentangle visual matching from instructor cues. • To establish sequences of *select, scan, match, select* • *Decide which things go together.*
Set up	• Place three plates on the table with a sample object on each. Have the child stand a few feet away from the table with a bin of objects next to the plates. The objects in the bin correspond to the objects on the plates (a minimum of two of each kind).
Procedure	1. Instruct the child to "sort" or provide another relevant cue. He should then match the objects, one by one, until the bin is empty. Provide manual guidance from behind and fade assistance over successive trials. 2. Gradually increase (a) the kinds of items on the table (up to a field of at least five), and (b) the number of items of each kind (up to at least four). (There is no magic number; the idea is simply to build toward greater proficiency). 3. Initially, the objects should be similar (identical).
Considerations	• Sorting may be implemented when the child is proficient with "Basic Matching"). • Sorting may have to be built from smaller steps; starting with two objects in each of two bins and only two corresponding objects (one on each of the plates). • Avoid verbal prompting. If the child deviates from the task, guide him back manually. • Ideally, sorting should be addressed at the same time as "Bring Same". Thus, the child will be expanding matching abilities across different contexts.

	Sorting (2)
Purpose	• To teach the child to organize items by kind without any environmental cues (pre-arranged sample). • To address basic inference and decision making.
Set up	• Place three plates on the table <u>without</u> a sample object on each. The child should stand a few feet from the table containing a bin of objects (a minimum of two of each kind; a total of six items).
Procedure	1. Instruct the child to "sort" or provide another relevant cue. He should pick one item from the bin and place it on an empty plate and then return to the bin and pick another item. If that second object corresponds to the object already on the plate, he should place it on that plate. If the object does not match, he should place it on an empty plate. This process continues until all the objects are sorted correctly. 2. Provide manual guidance from behind. 3. Increase the number of kinds of objects (plates) as the child becomes more proficient.
Considerations	• This is a challenging task for many children and success may not follow directly from "Sorting (1)" • This exercise deviates from conventional matching exercises as it does not offer explicit antecedent cues (presentation of an object as in "Basic Matching", or pre-arranged comparison fields (as in "Sorting 1". • If the child does not demonstrate progress within three to four sessions (i.e., manual guidance cannot be faded), the program should be postponed and re-introduced when progress is made in other matching programs such as "Find Same" and "Selection-Based Imitation".

	Bring Same
Purpose	<ul><li>To promote working memory (remember what you saw and go find it), sustained focus, persistent searching/problem solving, and basic social awareness.</li><li>To develop the routines of *look, search, return, and deliver.*</li><li>To combine basic matching, simple problem solving and basic social awareness.</li></ul>
Set up	<ul><li>Place items around the room.</li></ul>
Procedure	1. Hold up a picture and say: "Find same". The child should search for and retrieve the corresponding object. 2. After presenting the picture, guide the child to the corresponding object, assist him to pick it up and deliver it to you (use open hand cue). 3. If the child deviates from the task or loses track of what he is looking for (i.e., forgets), interrupt gently, bring him back to the point of origin and re-present the picture. 4. As progress is made, increase the distance and radius (spread) of the objects. The objects should be placed in different kinds of positions (on the floor, eye-level, and above eye-level such as on shelves). 5. With increased progress, make sure that the objects are more difficult to locate. At this level, the child may forget what he is looking for and may look back at you for information. If so, present the picture immediately. This "re-check" (information seeking) is a pivotal skill. 6. Make sure to also increase the distance between you and the child, and to vary your position relative to the child when presenting the instruction.

Considerations	• All the elements of the *look, search, return and deliver* routine should be addressed systematically and individually:
	• *Look:* Alter presenting the picture; hold it up in different positions so the child must strive to see it.
	• *Search:* Place objects in different kinds of positions (on the floor, eye-level, and above eye-level) and eventually partially (or fully hidden) so the child must manipulate the environment to find it (e.g., behind or in other objects).
	• *Return:* Initially, wait at the point of origin until the child returns with the object. When this routine is established, move yourself around (including out of sight) so that the child must strive to locate you.
	• *Deliver:* Initially, use an explicit open hand cue (prompt). As the child reliably delivers the object, discontinue the hand cue and require the child to 'capture your attention' (such as moving into your visual field, tapping your arm in, holding the object up in front of you). Such 'initiations' may be shaped in a systematic manner with the assistance of a second instructor who provides manual guidance from behind the child.

	Bring Same: Two Steps
Purpose	• To increase visual working memory, introduce multiple step instructions, motor planning/problem solving.
	• To expand "Bring Same".
Set up	• Place items around the room.
Procedure	1. Present a picture and say: "Get this" and wait for the child to find the corresponding object. When the child picks it up,

	present another picture and guide the child to pick up the second corresponding object. Use an open hand cue to prompt the child to hand you the objects. Initially, the objects should be in close proximity and easy to locate. 2. As the child demonstrates success, decrease the time between the picture presentations until they are presented in immediate succession and eventually, simultaneously.
Considerations	• The transition from single step to two-step may be challenging for some children and may require extensive practice. Be prepared that children often put down the first object when the second picture is presented. Prolonged practice involving only one object ("Bring Same") may amplify this problem, therefore transition to multiple steps should be made as soon as possible. • As progress is made, make sure that the objects are more difficult to locate (encourages searching). • The child may forget what he is looking for and look back at you for a reminder. Continue to display both pictures until the child has completed the two-step task).

	Touch Same
Purpose	• To further develop scanning, shifting attention, and working visual memory. • To shift modality of matching from handling objects/pictures (placing objects/pictures together, retrieving objects) to pointing.
Set up	• Place pictures on a table
Procedure	• Display a picture and instruct the child to "point to same". He should look at the picture, scan the pictures on the table,

	and point to the corresponding one. • With progress, you may (a) gradually reduce the time the picture is available (eventually just "flash" it), and (b) gradually increase the number of pictures on the table (extend scanning requirement). • Use conventional discrete trial instruction • If the child makes consecutive errors, decrease the field size or prime the child with conventional picture matching (see "Basic Matching", "Matching Objects to Pictures").
Considerations	• Discontinue conventional matching exercises when progress is made with this exercise. • Consider using pictures that are *slightly* dissimilar in order to enhance visual acuity (e.g., one car with white roof and one with black roof, two different kinds of dogs).

	Find Same
Purpose	• To further develop the executive function skills of working visual memory and searching. • To teach the child to seek information when they forget. • To establish appropriate eye contact. • To establish sequence of *look, search, point and check back.*
Set up	• Place a picture on each page in small binder or photo album.
Procedure	• Present a picture and tell the child to "find same." The child turns pages in the binder and points to the corresponding picture when it appears. Initially, use

12

	manual guidance.
	• As the child makes progress, you should withhold praise/reinforcement until he looks at you after pointing to the target picture.
	• Initially, the target picture should be on the first or second page. As the child makes progress, more pages should be added to the binder and the target picture should be placed further into the back. When extending the task this way, the child may forget which picture they are looking for and may therefore look back at you for information (communicating non verbally that the child seeks information). When looking back is becomes more regular, wait to present the picture until eye contact occurs (see also "Bring Same).
	• Use conventional discrete trial instruction.
Considerations	• As children look consistently to you for information, change the format: Rather than presenting a single picture, place an array of pictures on the table and point to one of them when giving the instruction "find same". When the child looks up to find out what you want them to 'find', wait for eye contact before pointing to the target picture. This is an iteration of SBI (below).
Troubleshooting	• Some children have difficulty turning the pages. Use thicker pages or tabs to make it easier.

	Selection-Based Imitation (SBI) (1)
Purpose	• To facilitate the development of pointing, flexible shift of attention, joint attention, and tracking.
	• Strengthen executive function.

Set up	• Sit directly across the child at the table. Both of you have a row of corresponding pictures. The two rows are arranged so the *pictures correspond in terms of position*. The rows may be arranged so both are oriented toward the child. • Begin with a field of three pictures and increase with success.
Procedure	1. Say: "Do this" and point to a picture in front of you. The child should then point to the corresponding picture in his row. 2. Use "Touch same" as a bridge to establish SBI: Instead of pointing to a picture, pick up a picture and say; "Touch same". As the child catches on, change from holding up a picture to pointing to one (on the table).
Considerations	• SBI is a 'tool skill' rather than a goal in itself. • SBI is a hybrid of matching and imitation and differs from conventional (typography-based) imitation. In selection-based imitation, the response is the same every time (pointing), while in conventional imitation, the response is different from instance to instance. SBI also differs from conventional imitation in that it requires elements of joint attention, shifting attention, increased memory load, and tracking. This is a complex social event. • SBI may serve as a tool for establishing "receptive object naming" (Lund, 2004) and may aid in development of imitation for children who struggle with conventional imitation training.

	Selection-Based Imitation (2)
Purpose	• To further develop pointing, flexible shift of attention, joint

	attention, and tracking.
	• A direct extension of "Selection-Based Imitation 1"
	• This version of SBI controls for the problem of positional prompts.
Set up	• Sit directly across the child at the table. Have a row of pictures in front of you and a corresponding row in front of him. Arrange the field so the *pictures <u>no longer correspond by position within the rows.</u>* The rows may be arranged so both are oriented toward the child (**see Figure 1**).
Procedure	• Say "do this" and point to a picture in your row. The child then points to the corresponding picture in his row.
Considerations	• The child may copy the position of your finger as opposed finding the target picture (e.g., if you point to the far-left picture, the child may do the same whether the pictures match or not) or he may first point to the picture corresponding to the position of your finger and then switch to the correct picture. To address these problems you could, (a) scale back to two pictures and increase the field size when the child performs proficiently, (b) block the child's response to permit sufficient scanning time. (For instance, the child's effort may be blocked until he observes your response and shifts attention to his own pictures) and (c) interrupt "position pointing" and introduce a new trial after a brief delay (two, three seconds).

Figure 1

	Selection-Based Imitation (3)
Purpose	• Same as SBI 2 with increased distance.
Set up	• Children have an array of pictures placed in front of them • On a board or wall several feet away are corresponding pictures.
Procedure	• Say: "do this" while pointing to a picture. The child should point to the corresponding picture in the array front of them.
Considerations	• Child and instructor are no longer 'knee to knee'. • Orientation to instructors from a distance is a critical ability and should be a natural extension across all exercises as appropriate.

	Selection-Based Imitation: Two Steps
Purpose	• To extend observational abilities, curb impulsive responding, and enhance working memory. • To teach sequential ordering.
Set up	• Same arrangement as "Selection-based imitation (2)".
Procedure	• Say: "do this" while pointing to a picture. Then say "and this" and point to another picture. The child should point to the corresponding pictures in his row. Use a shaping/time delay procedure: Point to the first picture and wait for the child to initiate his response. When he responds, point to the second picture. Keep your finger on the second picture until the child responds correctly. Increase the speed gradually as he is able to follow along.
Considerations	• Multi-step instruction is difficult for many children. Common problems include attention drift, impulsivity, and order conflation (i.e., reversing the order of stimulus input/pointing to the picture in the opposite order). This exercise is designed to improve these issues. • Establishing this skill often requires meticulous and creative shaping. Using the time delay procedure described above is an example of one shaping strategy. • If the child does not demonstrate progress after three to four sessions, the exercise may be postponed and reintroduced when the child demonstrates success with other multiple step exercises such as "Multi-Step Imitation" (see Imitation mini-manual) and "Bring Same: Two steps"..

	Sequential Matching (TPSM)
Purpose	<ul><li>To teach a multi-component sequence of *turn, point, select, match* (TPSM).</li><li>To strengthen executive functions including working memory, scanning, searching, and shifting attention between components of tasks.</li></ul>
Set up	<ul><li>Place on a table four to six pictures face down, in a row. Place a bin containing a set of corresponding items to the child's left (on a separate table or chair). **(Fig. 2).**</li></ul>
Procedure	1. The child should turn the first picture (T), point to it (P), select the corresponding item from the bin (S), and place it on the picture (M) **(Fig. 3)**. Continue until the child has completed all the matches (up to six pictures). 2. Assist (manual guidance) from behind until independent.
Considerations	<ul><li>Sequential matching or "Turn-Point-Select-Match" (TPSM) may be introduced when the child has mastered "Sorting "and "Matching Objects to Pictures".</li><li>TPSM is a 'tool' that may later be used to enable development of basic communication skills.</li><li>When the child performs fluently, omit the first part of the sequence. Thus, the pictures are placed face up. The child should then point (P), select the corresponding object (S), and match it (M).</li><li>As the child progresses, include items that are similar so that finer discriminations are required to make accurate matches.</li></ul>

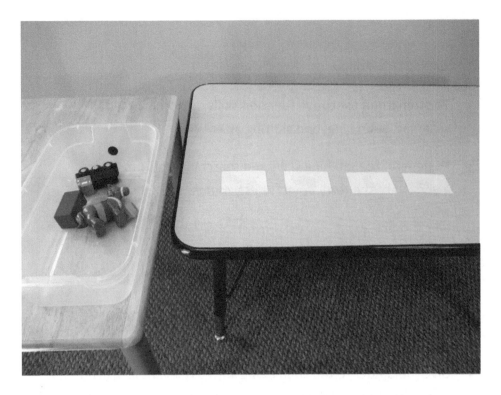

Fig. 2

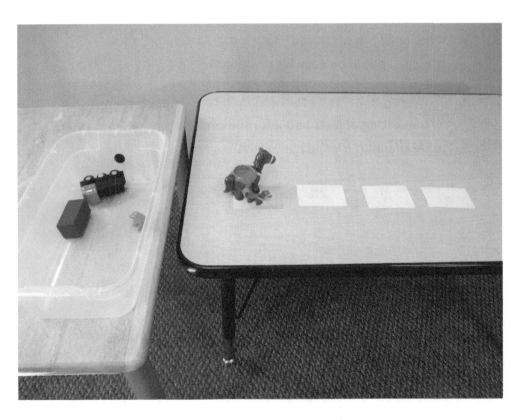

Fig 3

	Following Lists ("shopping")
Purpose	<ul><li>To strengthen executive function skills of working memory, scanning, searching, and shifting attention</li><li>To generalize matching skills and searching (this program is a version of the *turn, point, select, match*, see "Sequential Matching").</li><li>To strengthen task completion (independent problem solving).</li></ul>
Set up	<ul><li>Place familiar pictures in a binder (one on each page) and arrange corresponding objects around the room.</li></ul>
Procedure	<ul><li>Give the binder to the child along with a relevant instruction (e.g., "Do your schedule"). He should open the binder, point to the picture (can be omitted), retrieve the corresponding object, place it in a bin, turn to the next page, etc.</li></ul>
Considerations	<ul><li>If the child has mastered "Sequential Matching", this exercise should be easy for the child.</li><li>"Following Lists" is a tool used for later language goals such as requesting objects and information, teaching yes/no, and other pragmatic language exercises.</li></ul>

	Search (1)
Purpose	<ul><li>To develop persistent searching and exploration.</li><li>Teach the child to reposition himself and manipulate the environment to obtain objects.</li></ul>
Set up	<ul><li>Place three or more cups/containers on the table spaced far enough apart so it is not possible for the child to view their</li></ul>

	contents. • Place a highly preferred item in one of the cups.
Procedure	• Guide the child to each of the containers so he may see what is inside. When he encounters the cup with the preferred item allow him to take it. Fade guidance so the child eventually searches for the item independently.
Considerations	• When the child demonstrates proficiency, introduce more challenging tasks so that the child must use a variety of actions to gain access to the objects. For instance; use opaque containers so that the child needs to 'pour' out the contents to see what is inside, wrap things up so that the child needs to pull things apart to see what is inside, use nested items (e.g., a small paper bag inside closed containers), or place items in an opaque container (bag, box) that allows an item's removal only if child reaches in and pulls it out. • Keep in mind the importance of teaching children to problem-solve as opposed to requesting assistance. While requesting help and assistance is a critical target, it should not overshadow development of practical problem solving. Be alert to the 'passivity fallacy' in which the child routinely defers attempts to problem solve and explore.

	Search (match 1)
Purpose	• To develop search routines, memory.
Set up	• An opaque container which contains several items.
Procedure	• Visually, present a matched item which, corresponds to one

	of those in the container, and ask the child to find same. • Manually guide • Fade guidance
Considerations	• Limit to two, the number of items in box until the child is independent and then increase the number • Use easily 'recognizable' items e.g., a ball, a block, a book.

	Search (match 2)
Purpose	• To develop search routines, memory.
Set up	• Two opaque containers. • In one is only one item (box a). • In the other are several items, one of which matches the item in the other container (box b).
Procedure	Instruct the child to 'find out what is in the box' (box a). Guide the child to reach in, feel for the item but to not remove it. Direct child to 'find same' in the other box. Guide the child to reach into the other.
Considerations	• Use easily 'recognizable' items e.g., a ball, a block, a book. • Limit to two, the number of items in box b until the child is independent and then increase the number. • This exercise is an extension of "Touch same" and "Find

	same".

Imitation

	Gross Motor Imitation
Purpose	To teach the child to observe and copy another person's simple gross motor movements.
Set up	Sit face to face.
Procedure	1. Say: "Do this" and simultaneously model a simple movement. Prompt the corresponding movement immediately (manual guidance). Fade prompts over successive trials. 2. Use conventional discrete trial instruction. 3. Start with simple gross motor movements such as waving, clapping, touching head, raising arms, and eventually introduce 'out of the chair' movements such as walking around the chair and running. 4. When the child masters a particular movement, introduce another and randomize it with mastered ones. Continue to introduce novel movements until the child imitates new ones without specific training.
Considerations	• Establishing imitation may require considerable repetition with extensive manual guidance. • Child may often 'jump the Sd' and not wait for the presentation of the model. It may be necessary to gently holds the child's hands in their own laps with your one hand, while presenting the model with your other hand. Once the model is presented, prompt to match the imitative model. • For some children, it is easier to learn gross motor imitation when using objects (see "Object Imitation 1). • Once imitation is established 'knee to knee', present models when 'standing face to face'. Standing with instructors will be required throughout much of intervention and should begin as early as possible.
Troubleshooting	• If the child is not making progress, it may be necessary to strengthen subservient skills such as shifting attention, sustained attention, and working memory. These skills are

	addressed systematically in various matching programs ("Basic Identity Matching" "Sequential Matching, "Selection-Based Imitation"). • Also, consider placing a strong reinforcer in your hand. Model a movement (e.g., touch head, touch belly). using only the hand with reinforcer in it. As your hand moves it's likely the child will track it (You'll know it's a strong reinforcer if the child tracks). Move slowly, pacing your hand movement as the child tracks its movement. If the child tracks all the way through the movement, prompt. Fade prompts and increase speed over successive trials.

	Fine Motor Imitation
Purpose	• To teach the child to attend to and imitate fine motor movements, facial expressions (including mouth movements). • Strengthen observational acuity /fine tune child's attention to small differences in movements.
Set up	Sit face to face.
Procedure	1. Say: "Do this" and simultaneously model a simple movement. Prompt the corresponding action immediately (manual guidance). Fade prompts over successive trials. 2. Use conventional discrete trial instruction. 3. Start with simple fine motor movements such as pointing, thumbs up, folding hands, and putting index fingers together. 4. Once the child masters a particular movement, introduce another and randomize it with mastered ones. 5. Continue to introduce novel movements until the child imitate new ones without specific training.
Considerations	• If the child struggles, use more salient targets and then, over time, increase subtlety. • Functional targets may also be considered such as using glue sticks, forks, spoons, use of playdoh to make simple things the

	child might enjoy making etc.
	• Movements such as shaking and nodding head sometimes need to be taught specifically and should be considered before starting "yes" and "no" so that you may be able to pair the gestures with their corresponding words.

	Multi-Step Imitation
Purpose	• To expand imitation skills. • To reproduce a sequence of movements in the order they were observed. • To exercise executive function skills such as ordering of motor skills (motor planning), working memory and the suppression of incorrect pre-potent responding.
Set up	Sit face to face.
Procedure	• Say "do this" and model two movements. The movements should be distinctly different (e.g., clap and wave) and presented consecutively with minimal time delay. Upon completion of the sequenced model, the child should perform them in the order they were presented.
Considerations	• Multi-step imitation requires the child to, (a) observe compound movements (sustained attention to transient events), (b) remember the sequence (movements and their order), and (c) refrain from copying the last movement until he performs the first (impulse suppression). • The step from single step to two-step imitation is dramatic and extensive practice is often necessary.
Troubleshooting	• _The child_ imitates only the first movement and/or responds to the first movement before observing the second. To address this problem, have a second person provide prompts from behind. The second person should prevent (physical blocking) the child from responding until both movements are presented. Also, consider postponing the exercise and

	establish or strengthen "Selection-Based Imitation: Two Steps" then re-introduce.
	• If a second person is not available, gently hold the child's hand in their lap while you present the two step movements and prompt immediately following the presentation.
	• *The child* imitates only the second movement. To address this problem, slow things down, i.e., present the first movement and when the child imitates it, introduce the second. Increase the speed gradually. If the problem persists, it may be helpful to establish multi-step imitation with objects (see "Object imitation 2") before returning to this exercise. Also, consider postponing the exercise and establish or strengthen "Selection-Based Imitation: Two Steps", then re-introduce.
	• It also me be helpful, to have the child "shadow" your movements.
	• *The child* reverses the order. To address this problem, practice segments in which you present the first movement, wait for the child to imitate and then present the second. Also, consider postponing the exercise and establish or strengthen "Selection-Based Imitation: Two Steps"), then re-introduce. Fluency with "Sequential Matching" may also aid the child with this difficulty.

	Object Imitation (1)
Purpose	• To see that the child learns to observe and copy another person's simple actions with objects.
Set up	• Face each other; two sets of identical objects are separated on the child's table.
Procedure	• Say "do this" while picking up an item and manipulating it in a particular way (e.g., placing it in a particular location, banging it, turning it). The child should select the corresponding object and imitate the movement.

27

	• Arrange 'distracter objects' (extra objects which won't be used) to ensure discrimination. For instance, if you put a block in a bucket, there should be a block and one additional object for the child to choose from. Increase the number of objects as the child demonstrates success.
Considerations	• Start with simple actions such as putting a block in a bucket, peg in pegboard, banging the table with a hammer, etc. • Upon success with simple actions, introduce more complex ones. For instance, turning a cup upside down and putting a block inside, taking apart two pop-beads and placing them in a bucket, taking a peg out of the pegboard and banging it on the table. • It is important that objects are not always used in the same manner. For instance, a hammer should not always be used to bang the table, but sometimes placed in the bucket, slid on the floor etc. Likewise, a block can be used to bang the table rather than placed in a bucket. This will prevent memorization of object-action sequences and compels the child to observe the entire action every time. • Some children have an easier time learning imitation with objects before imitation without objects.

	Object Imitation (2)
Purpose	• To expand the child's ability to observe and copy another person's actions with objects.
Set up	• _Multiple steps:_ Two sets of identical objects on the child's table. • _Distance and delay_: Two sets of identical objects are spread out on the floor.
Procedure	• _Multiple-steps_: Both of you and the child have a set of corresponding objects. Say; "do this" and manipulate an object, then say "and this" while manipulating another. After the last movement, the child should imitate both in the order

28

	presented. Start with simple combinations such as *block in a bucket + bang the table with a hammer*; *put a peg in a peg-board + turn a cup upside down*; *unsnap two pop-beads + roll a car across the table.* • *Distance and delay:* Both of you should each have a set of corresponding objects. The child's objects are placed on the floor, out of reach and out of the immediate visual field (peripherally). Say "do this" while picking up an item and manipulating it in a particular way (e.g., placing it in a particular location, banging it, turning it). The child should then *search for* the corresponding object and imitate the movement.
Considerations	*Multiple-steps:* • Common problems: Similar to "Multi-Step Imitation" If the child continues to struggle, consider postponing the exercise and establish or strengthen "Selection-Based Imitation: Two Steps then re-introduce. Fluency with "Sequential Matching" • may also help the child with this exercise. • As the child makes progress with this program, omit the second verbal cue ("and this"). Thus, say; "do this" and then model two consecutive movements. • This exercise may serve as a bridge to "Follow the Leader" and "Observational Learning". *Distance and delay:* • This task is quite challenging for many children and must be built up gradually (i.e., incremental changes in the objects position relative to the child). • When the child masters this exercise, combine it with "multiple-steps".

	Block Imitation – Step by Step
Purpose	• To teach block building and strengthen imitation skills. • To refine visual-motor coordination and establish "triadic attention shift": Shifting attention systematically from model to set of blocks to own structure. This sequence of *Look, select, construct, check back* is essential to advanced skill learning. • To foster development of spatial awareness, and visual perspective taking. • To increase searching and scanning, and develop early understanding of part-whole relations. • To establish block building as a platform for teaching language and problem-solving abilities.
Set up	• Sit next to each other at a table. You each have a set of colored wood blocks which includes distracters.
Procedure	• Place one of the blocks, from your pile on the table in front of the child, and say: "do this". The child needs to select the corresponding block from their own pile and place it in front of your block (When done, you should select another block and place it on top of the first (**Fig. 4**). The child does the same. Use manual guidance if necessary. • Once the two-block sequence is mastered, gradually increase the number of blocks to seven or eight. • Start with simple vertical structures and make the structures increasingly more complex over time.
Considerations	• Initially, the child should build his structure just below the model. When he does well, start building side-by-side. • If the child struggles, focus on "Selection-Based Imitation" in order to promote flexible shift of attention between sets of objects. • Block imitation and block building are crucial to development of core cognitive skills and will be used extensively in later language building exercises.
Trouble-shooting	• If the child selects the wrong block from his own pile: Strengthen "Object Imitation and return to the exercise. Alternatively, line the blocks up in a corresponding fashion so it is easier for the

	child to discern the correct one.
	• If the child places the block in the wrong position:
	Slow down the pace and simplify the structure. In the initial phases of this exercise, do not challenge the child with subtle positions or orientation (e.g., placing a block in the middle of a base block versus at the edge) and the aspect of blocks (standing up versus lying flat).
	• If the child continues to build his structure using 'distracter' blocks: Provide mass trials and abruptly interrupt upon completion of the model (and reinforce of course).

Fig 4

	Block Imitation - From completed model
Purpose	• To move from step-by-step imitation to copy a pre-built structure. • To establish the ability to 'keep track' of progression within a complex task', and to further establish "triadic attention shift" (*look, select, construct, check back*).

Set up	• Sit next to each other at a table. Build a block structure (out of colored wood blocks) behind a barrier and then reveal it. The child has a set of blocks, including distractors.
Procedure	1. Instruct the child to build the model revealed. (**Fig. 5**) Provide manual guidance if necessary. 2. Start with a two-block structure (a base block and one other). For some children it may be helpful to begin with a stationary base block (a block placed in front of the child before revealing the model. The base block marks the starting point. 3. Start with only one "distracter". It is critical for the child to learn to omit the extra block. This can be challenging and it may be useful for child to place the extra block on a designated area (i.e., a plate). As he becomes successful, more distracters can be introduced. 4. Gradually increase the number of blocks and the complexity in the structures (i.e., from straight towers to more complex three-dimensional arrangements).
Considerations	• The change from step-by-step imitation to copying pre-built structures may require gradual transitions. For instance, you may need to extend step-by-step building by incrementally speeding up the modeling process from discrete building (one block at a time and wait for the child to complete the effort) to continuous building (introducing the next block right before the child completes the first block). • The cognitive challenges involved in copying pre-built structures are many and include, flexible and systematic shift of attention between three domains (the model, an array of blocks, and own construction), comparison between two structures and discerning discrepancies, tracking progress/continuous tracking (knowing which step is current and which step has been completed), motor planning, and eye-hand coordination. As the block structures become more complex, so do the challenges; depth perception, judging and probing distance between blocks (how close do two pillars have to be to support a "roof"?), judging which block to build first (foundation versus subsequent blocks, understanding the concept of "support"), correcting detected errors, fine-grained adjustments to make things fit, discerning aspect (e.g., is

the block lying flat or standing up, is it aligned or across), and position (e.g., is the block in the middle of another or at the edge? Is it set back or in the foreground of its base?).

- All these actions will also be considered in language instruction, so it is important to cover these actions as fully as possible in these imitation exercises.

- This exercise challenges motor-planning abilities. Some children pick up a block with each hand and have subsequent difficulties coordinating/sequencing their actions. It may be necessary to prompt the child to pick up one block at the time (i.e., gently block the less dominant hand).

Fig. 5

	Block Imitation 3d from 2d
Purpose	• To advance imitation of pre-built block structures. • To relate three-dimensional to two-dimensional structures • To ensure that the child is able to relate complex stimuli of different dimensions and scale.
Set up	• Sit next to each other at a table with pictures of different kinds of block structures and a corresponding set of blocks.
Procedure	1. Present a picture of a block structure and say: "Do this" (or "build this"). The child should build a corresponding structure with his own set of blocks. 2. Gradually increase the number of blocks and complexity of the structure (i.e., from "vertical" to more complex three-dimensional arrangements).
Considerations	• Before starting this exercise, children should be fluent with building from completed models. • Being able to build from 2d models will be useful if considering use of activity schedules.

	Follow the Leader
Purpose	• To advance imitation skills and continuous tracking of other person's movements.
Set up	• Natural environments.
Procedure	1. Say: "Do this" (or "follow me" or "do what I do") and perform a simple movement that may or may not involve an object (e.g., clapping versus knocking on the door). The child should imitate the movement and you move about the room and model additional movements. 2. Place a strong emphasis on imitation that involves objects (kicking a ball, walking around a table, throwing a bean bag, etc.).

	3. Initially, the instruction "do this" may be presented before each movement (a more discrete format), but as the child becomes fluent, the verbal instruction should be presented only at the beginning of the sequence.
	4. Gradually increase the length of the imitation segments. Start with two movements.
Considerations	• This exercise represents a break from a discrete trial format and requires sustained and flexible shift of attention.
	• A reasonable goal is a four to five step sequence.
	• This exercise may facilitate following models from videos.
	• Once fluent, introduce activities such as dance, calisthenics, yoga, group movement activities etc. anything the child finds enjoyable.

	Oral Motor Imitation
Purpose	• To establish oral-motor imitation.
Set up	• Sit face to face.
Procedure	• Present the instruction *"Do this"*
	• Consider targets such as opening and closing mouth, licking lips, puffing out cheeks, smacking lips, blowing air (use bubbles too) etc.
Considerations	• Oral motor imitation will be important as children learn to make words. Attention to what others do to make those sounds is an obvious critical requirement.
	• This, of course, requires that children look at our faces. Early on, children need to develop a habit of looking at us, meeting our gazes and scanning our faces. The developmental literature is clear that child who meet the eyes of others also spend much of their time scanning faces (see discussion related to current trends related to 'teaching eye contact). If children are not looking at our faces, shaping sounds will be much more

	difficult since much visual information will be missed.

	Verbal Imitation
Purpose	To establish vocal imitation.
Set up	Sit face to face.
Procedure	• Present the instruction _"Say"_ followed by a target sound, word or sentence. The target sound should (a) be presented slightly louder that than _"say"_ and (b) there should be a short delay (one second) between _"Say"_ and the target sound. (For additional consideration about how to establish, "say", as a controlling antecedent stimulus go to www.nexusais.com/the-clumsy-echoic. • Initially, any approximation to the target sound should be reinforced. • Increase complexity/length of vocalizations with increasing success.
Considerations	• Verbal imitation should be considered when the child is focusing well on their teachers and competent with basic imitation. • While we refer to this exercise as "Verbal Imitation", it is really to teach children to follow the instruction to 'say what we say' when _instructed_ to do so; this is NOT to teach echoics. • Verbal imitation, just as oral motor imitation requires that children look at our faces. • We also like to wait until the child begins to imitate sounds or words spontaneously (without effort or direct intervention). We often see this occur following the commencement of receptive label exercises or receptive instruction exercises. ○ However, such repetitive imitation can result in echolalia and it is therefore important that verbal imitation comes under conditional antecedent control as soon as possible (see next bullet point). • Initially, the child may imitate "say" and it may be tempting to

	omit this instruction. However, verbal imitation training that omits "say" could induce or perpetuate echolalia. It is imperative that verbal imitation is brought under the conditional stimulus control of the instruction "say". While sometimes the instructor may omit "say" in the very beginning, this conditional cue must be introduced as soon as the child begins to imitate sounds. • While this early introduction to verbal imitation is critical, 'verbal imitation' is a tool that is used to throughout intervention. It is used to help children increase mean length utterance and such practice is encouraged. It is be used to prepare children for 'asking questions'… so that before initiating exercises for "asking" make sure children can follow the "say" instruction, i.e., that they will say what they are instructed to say rather than attempt to answer what may be perceived as a question. • When children reliably imitate words or approximations to words, expressive naming1 should be considered. • For a discussion concerning the use of 'echoics' vs use of conditional antecedent control, go to www.nexusais.com/the-clumsy-echoic .

	Grapho-Motor Imitation
Purpose	• To establish grapho-motor imitation.
Set up	• Stand behind the child.
Procedure	• Present the instruction "Do this" or "Draw this", and draw a straight line. • Prompt the child from behind to pick up the writing implement and to match what you've drawn.
Considerations	• There are two components involved here. Proper grasp of the writing tools and the writing itself. • A useful prompting strategy for proper grasp is to have the

	child use a pincer grasp to pick up the implement. With their other hand, they can learn to 'push' the implement back so that it is cradled nicely between the thumb and forefinger. Hand-over-hand prompting is required here. • The second part of course is to teach children how to use the implement. We recommend starting with dry erase markers since less pressure is required so feedback is immediate. We like to have two large dots on a dry erase board. Prompt the child to 'connect the dots' and to lift the marker when they reach the second dot. But individualize these early steps as you see fit. • If necessary, teach each component separately and then combine. • Once basic line drawing is established, begin to introduce more complex imitative tasks still using straight lines, e.g., connect lines to form the letter "L" or rectangles or squares etc. Then begin curved lines and representations of things like cars, trains, trees etc. • Consider teaching children to copy from completed pictures. We recommend trying the Ed Emberley Drawing Books once certain proficiencies are established. • Consider combining 'matching' and 'graphomotor' abilities as quickly as possible in worksheet activities; these can eventually be incorporated in activity schedules. • Additional 'worksheet' activities such as 'dot – dot' should be considered as quickly as possible as well. •

	Third Person Imitation
Purpose	• To address aspects of imitation, tracking and flexible shift of attention. • To break away from a one-to-one teaching format. • To address an emergent understanding of pointing and the deixis "this" and "that".

38

Set up	• Two instructors are required for this exercise.
Procedure	• Point to another person and say; "do that" or "do like [name]". The child should imitate the movement of the second person. Deliver the cue ("do that" + point) and guide the child manually to attend to the other person. Initially, the second person may be in the child's immediate visual field (i.e., next to you). • Randomize "do that" (imitating second person) and "do this" (imitating you). • With progress, alternate your role and second person's role.
Considerations	• This is a later imitation program. The child must be able to track (follow a point), track the movement of others and demonstrate the ability to "Follow the Leader". • Many children have difficulty shifting from one model to another. Extensive practice is often necessary. If the child shows persistent difficulty, postpone this exercise and strengthen tracking and observational learning (next exercise). With progress in these areas, reinstatement should be considered. • Third person imitation is a crucial ability and is essential to further social and language development. It involves (1) the basic deixis of "this" and "that", (2) the ability to track and to sustain attention to events at a distance, (3) conditions which promote understanding of speaker roles (i.e., a person's role shifts, speakers provide information and gives directives). • If children have difficulty with this exercise, consider returning to selection-based imitation (2)(3) in order to ensure that children are fully focused on activity of instructors.

	Observational Learning
Purpose	• To teach children to observe others and imitate the actions of others at a later time. For instance, the child observes an action in one location, and imitates it in a different location or when a

	similar situation requires a similar action. • To strengthen working memory and problem solving (i.e., using information obtained at one point in time at a later time).
Set up	Natural environment, familiar objects.
Procedure	• Model an action with an object then guide the child to a different location where he has access to the same kind of problem. The child should imitate the action at the second location in order to solve the problem (e.g., use some object as a tool). • Start with very short distances. For instance, model an action at a table, then turn the child around to face another table that contains the relevant objects. Increase the distance to the second table gradually.
Considerations	• The child should be able to "Follow the Leader" and perform multi step imitation with objects. "True" observational learning, in which the child imitates actions after a considerable time delay, (e.g., sees something at school and imitates at home) is not likely to follow automatically from this exercise. Rather, this exercise is designed to <u>begin</u> the process of developing observational learning. • Once the child develops basic observational learning, numerous opportunities should be provided throughout the day. In other words, observational learning must become a regular feature of the child's everyday environment.

Early Receptive Language

	One Step Instructions
Purpose	To teach children to follow simple directions.
Set Up	Sit or stand facing each other.
Procedure	1. Present an instruction (e.g., "clap") and manually guide the child's response. Repeat the instruction and fade the prompt over successive trials. 2. When the child responds independently, introduce a second instruction and follow the same procedure. Randomize the first and the second instruction. 3. Introduce new instructions when the child discriminates between the two initial instructions.
Considerations	• Some children are more successful when two or more instructions are randomized from the outset. • Mastered instructions should eventually be introduced in less contrived settings. Alter dimensions such as location, setting, and proximity to the instructor. • Proficiency with programs like "tracking" (see tracking mini-manual) and "Selection Based Imitation" (see matching mini-manual) may facilitate development of receptive instruction. • A small subset of children struggles to learn simple receptive language. In some cases, it may be wise to postpone receptive language training and strengthen "tool" skills such as scanning, tracking, and working visual memory (see "Selection Based Imitation" in Matching mini-manual). • Some children learn to name objects expressively before receptively

	Two Step Instructions
Purpose	• To teach the child to follow two-part instructions. • To develop executive function skills such as ordering of motor responses, suppressing pre-potent but incorrect responding (impulsivity) and working memory.
Set up	• Sit face to face.
Procedure	1. Instruct the child to do two distinct things using the conjunction *"and"* (e.g., "clap" and "wave"). After the last instruction is presented, the child should do them in the order they were presented. 2. Initially, you may need to present the first instruction (e.g., "clap") and wait for the child to respond before introducing the next ("…and wave"). As he develops fluency with this sequence, instructions may be presented without time delay.

	Say versus Do (1)
Purpose	• To teach the child to differentiate between the instructions "Say [name of the object]" versus "Point to/Where is [name of the object]?" Example: "Say cup" versus "Point to the cup"?
Set up	• Sit face to face by a table with familiar items.
Procedure	• Randomize the instructions "Say [name of the object]" and "Point to/Where is [name of the object]?"
Considerations	• This exercise involves *conditional instructions* (Say the word only if you hear the word "say", otherwise point to the object corresponding to the word). These "if-but-not-otherwise" conditions may be quite difficult to learn and will often require additional practice before the ability solidifies (see "Receptive Colors: Conditional Discrimination" (See Mini-Manual: Colors, Shapes Size).

	• Mastery of "Say versus do" is necessary in order to address complex language abilities such as asking questions, using pronouns, giving direction etc. • Say vs. Do is an extension of verbal imitation (see verbal imitation in ABA mini-manual: Imitation.

	Say versus Do (2)
Purpose	• To teach the child to discriminate between following; the direction to 'say the action word' vs 'perform the action'. Example: "Say clap" versus "clap".
Set up	• Sit face to face.
Procedure	• Randomize the instructions "Say [action]" and "[action]".
Considerations	• As with "Say versus Do (1), this exercise involves *conditional instructions* (say the word only if you hear the word "say", otherwise perform the corresponding action). • This "if-but-not-otherwise" condition tends to be more difficult than "Say [object name]" versus "Point to the [object]". • Without the ability to discriminate these conditions, the child will not be able to move beyond labeling and rote responding. This is a "bottleneck" that the child must get through.
Troubleshooting	• If the child has difficulty with this exercise, it is often helpful to present a non-sense sound e.g., 'blinky blinky' / i.e., something that the child cannot do but can only say. Thus, alternate "Say, blinky- blinky" with you saying, "Blinky-blinky. When "Blinky-Blinky" is presented, the child should not do anything (there is nothing to do). If the child attempts to imitate (echo) "blinky-blinky", place a finger in front of the child's mouth (not necessarily to touch). If no echo is

	emitted, add strong reinforcer immediately. Continue until the instruction "say" exerts the desired result.

	Receptive Object Identification
Purpose	• To teach the child the names of common objects.
Set up	• Three objects on a table separated by a few inches.
Procedure	1. Use instructions such as "Where is [object]?", "Give me [object]" or "Find [object]". 2. Prompt by guiding the child's hand to the object and fade prompts over successive trials (conventional discrete trial instruction).
Considerations	• Object identification concerns the act of "mapping" words to concrete things; it is the basic element of symbolic or referential understanding. • In contrast to receptive *instructions*, object identification requires that the child scan an array of objects rather than perform a specific motor program. In this sense, receptive object labeling is "selection-based" rather than topography-based (based on form). • Many children struggle with identifying objects and may demonstrate inconsistency even after considerable teaching. It may be helpful to omit extra words in early instructions (i.e., simply "cup" as opposed to "find cup", etc.). If problems persist the exercise should be discontinued and an emphasis should be placed on strengthening "tool skills" such as scanning, shifting attention, tracking, and working memory within 'matching' exercise formats. • Some children learn expressive object naming before receptive language and the former may serve as a tool to teaching the latter.

	<ul><li>Use multiple exemplars (many different cars, many different balls, etc.).</li><li>As the child demonstrates proficiency with the basic arrangements, alter different aspects of the instructional setting by (a) increasing the field size to expand scanning and searching, (b) broaden the radius; displaying objects on a wider radius around the child (see "Bring Same), and (c) requested objects are hidden behind barriers, in drawers, under containers, etc. in order to strengthen searching routines.</li></ul>

	2-D Object Identification
Purpose	<ul><li>To expand receptive object identification.</li></ul>
Set up	<ul><li>Three pictures on a table separated by a few inches.</li></ul>
Procedure	1. Use instructions such as "Where is [object]?", "Show me [object]" or "Find [object]". 2. Prompt by guiding the child's hand to the appropriate picture and fade prompts over successive trials (conventional discrete trial instruction).
Considerations	<ul><li>The child should have mastered "Matching Objects to Pictures" and be able to identify several 3D objects.</li><li>Use multiple exemplars (many different cars, many different balls, etc.).</li><li>Object identification is a foundation for development of other language skills.</li></ul>
Additional steps and permutations	<ul><li>With success, introduce different formats: (a) Place a picture on each page in small binder or photo album. Ask the child to "find the [picture]". He should turn the pages and point to the target picture when it appears (see "Find Same for description); (b) use a typical picture book and ask the child</li></ul>

	to identify objects he knows, (c) place pictures upside down and ask the child for one of them. The child should then turn the pictures over until he finds the correct one, point to it and make look to the instructor. • Receptive object identification is the most basic form of word-world relation and is a foundation for expanding to words that denote relations between concrete things or events. Such terms are often referred to as "abstract" and include concepts such as prepositions and temporal relations (e.g., before/after) (e.g., Lovaas, 1977). While it is often necessary to elaborate and expand receptive object identification meticulously, abstract terms may be introduced once the student demonstrates reliable acquisition. Basic prepositions (see prepositions mini-manual) such as *on*, *in* and *under* are practical starting points for entry into abstract relations (cf. Lovaas, 1977).

	Receptive Person Identification
Purpose	• To identify familiar persons.
Set up	• A minimum of two familiar persons in addition to the instructor.
Procedure	• Instruct the child to "go to" [person]?" and then guide him to the corresponding person. The target person provides feedback (reinforcement). You then guide the child back to the point of origin. Fade prompts over successive trials as discrimination between two persons emerges.

Considerations	• Identifying persons requires the act of "mapping" names to persons. This differs from identifying objects in several important ways: (a) as opposed to objects, persons do not have a generic nature; persons are individuals and not an example or an instance of a concept, (b) face recognition and object recognition involves different neurological systems. Some children have significant difficulty learning names of persons although they are able to identify many objects, (c) while objects like cups, books and balls have distinct and unique "interaction properties" persons do not, (d) teaching persons names based on pictures is not a good substitute • Once the child learns the names of a few persons, pictures may be introduced. Pictures should eventually vary in size, angle, background, and focus.

	Responds to Name
Purpose	• To teach child to orient to others when their name is called. • To get the child's attention when they are not in the immediate vicinity or engaged in an activity.
Set up	• Natural environment. • Not recommended to teach this at the child's 'lessons' table.
Procedure	1. Call the child's name. 2. Make sure you are within arm's length. Immediately, after calling child's name, present, in the palm of your hand, an identified strong reinforcer (an eye catcher; see https://www.epmagazine.com/blog/keeping-it-fun-cutting-edge-social-skills-instruction-in-young-children-with-autism) bring it to your eyes and reinforcement immediately.

Considerations	• As children begin to orient more readily, increase the distance between you and the child when calling their name. Use of reinforcement and using an 'eye catcher' to orient will still be required except you will need to travel quickly to the child both to reinforce or to prompt as necessary. • "Responds to name" should not be conflated with 'come here'. • It is not necessary; in fact, we do not want children coming to us each time their name is called. Doing so will interfere with establishing conditions to teach child to do things, when requested, and they are not in close proximity. • The issue pertaining to "eye contact" has become controversial. A *careful* reading on this topic may allay some concern. For a discussion regarding this issue go to https://www.nexusais.com/teach-eye-contact-the-controversy .
Additional steps and permutations	• When the child is proficient with "Say vs. Do", consider teaching the child to say "what" or "yes" (you can include that they use the speakers name (e.g., "What Mommy) when their name is called. Begin to require this across rooms when the speaker in not in view. This exercise sets up conditions which allow you to begin making requests or asking questions of the child, and ensures that you have their attention. E.g., Call name>child says 'what Mommy">Can you bring me your backpack? Such permutations extend and integrate "bring me" and "responds to name".

	Responds to "Come Here"
Purpose	• To teach child to come to you when they are instructed to do so.
Set up	• Natural environment. • Stand a few feet from the child.

48

	• It is easier if there is a second person to assist in prompting.
Procedure	1. Say "Come here". 2. Manually guide the child to where you are. 3. Present reinforcement and eventually fade prompts.
Considerations	• Increase the distance; eventually from across rooms. • Change your position from where you make the request. • Eventually make yourself more difficult to find (stand behind walls, crouch behind a couch) so that the child will learn to search for you. • Once the child reliably comes when requested while indoors, begin to introduce outdoors. Be mindful of any safety concerns and it may be best to attempt this in an enclosed back yard if there are such concerns.

	Receptive Body Part Identification
Purpose	• To teach the child to identify their own and others' body-parts. • Rudimentary apprehension of part-whole concepts.
Set up	• Sit face to face.
Procedure	1. Instruct the child to "point to" or "touch" a body part and prompt the correct response. Fade prompts over successive trials. 2. When the child can identify two body parts, introduce new ones systematically.
Considerations	• Start with the most salient body parts such as head, tummy, foot, knee, nose, etc.
Additional steps and	• This exercise should eventually be extended to (a) identification of body parts of persons in pictures, (b)

permutations	identifying animal body parts.

	Receptive Block Building
Purpose	• To advance basic receptive language. • To teach the child to build things 'from memory'.
Set up	• Sit with the child at a table with colored wood blocks.
Procedure	1. Instruct the child to build a simple structure (e.g., "Make a house"). You should then guide him to build the structure. Fade assistance over successive trials. Initially, provide only the blocks needed for the target structure. 2. When the child has learned to build a particular structure, introduce another one. Teach the new structure in isolation and then randomize the first and the second structures. 3. Relevant prompting strategies include manual guidance, modeling, and reverse chaining.
Considerations	• The treatment team should agree on the exact form of each structure (e.g., Figs. below) • This program may be introduced when the child can imitate several complex pre-built block structures, and can easily identify several objects. • When teaching a new structure, the child should be given the required blocks only. Additional ("distracter blocks") should be introduced once he can build structures independently.

50

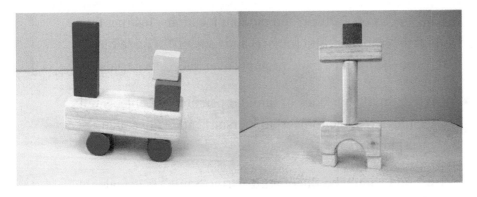

Train   *Person*

Bench

	Two-Step Receptive Objects
Purpose	• To teach the child to follow two-part instructions which incorporate additional abilities.
Set up	• See "Receptive Object Identification", "One step instruction" Two steps instructions), and "Bring Same".
Procedure	• *Object ID:* Arrange known objects or pictures on a table and say "point to [object] and [object]". Assist by pointing or using hand over hand guidance. Fade assistance over successive trials. • *Bring me:* Place objects around the room (those the child has learned to identify). Places should include proper locations

	(e.g., books on shelves) and random locations. Instruct the child to "bring me/find [object] and [object]". Guide him to retrieve the objects. Fade prompts over successive trials. • Give to: In the presence of familiar persons and objects tell the child "Give the [object] to [person]" and "Give a/an [object] to [person]".
Considerations	• The child should be fluent with "Bring Same" (see matching mini-manual, "Multiple Step Imitation" (see Imitation mini-manual) and "Two Step Instruction". • Some children may be successful with one of these formats (e.g., "Bring Same") but struggle with the other. The order of which to introduce these formats must be based on individual assessment.

	Gender Match-Receptive Follow-up
Purpose	• To match and identify by gender. • To demonstrate an additional teaching strategy when traditional object identification teaching strategies are ineffective.
Set up	• Place two plates on the table with sample pictures of a boy in one, a girl in the other.
Procedure	• Hand the child a picture of a different boys/girls and say "boys" or "girls" accordingly. • Provide manual guidance and fade assistance over successive trials. • As the child begins to match reliably, immediately following their correct match and say "Find boys" or "Find Girls" or some similar instruction. Prompt the child to touch that which they just matched.

Considerations	• Make sure to switch position of the items on the table regularly.
	• Many children often struggle learning the names of numbers, letters, colors, and persons. This teaching strategy of sort >receptive follow-up can be helpful in such situations.
	• Identification of "man", "woman" also will need to considered.
	• Naming by 'gender' will be eventually be required in relation to 'who' questions when names of individuals are not known. Thus, it is important to establish this receptively early in programing if language learning is to advance. Additionally, use of identification by gender is bound up with pronoun use.

Joint Attention

	Tracking 1
Purpose	• To teach the child to track/retrieve objects based on pointing. To develop a *'track-search-attain attention' sequence* as a fundamental social routine that *should be developed along* with *listen-search-attain attention* ("Bring Same in Matching Mini-manual). • To teach *a rudimentary understanding* of the deictic word "this".
Set up	• Line up a set of pictures and/or place pictures on a wall. Corresponding items are placed around the room.
Procedure	1. Point to one of the pictures and say: "Find this". The child needs to attend (track), locate the object, and give it to you 2. Start by touching the picture with your index finger and gradually increase the distance so that your touch becomes a point. Do not increase the distance beyond a reachable level (i.e., you should be able to reach the picture if you stretch your arm). 3. If the child can identify 2-D objects, the current arrangement should be alternated (i.e., "find this" while pointing to picture versus "find [object]").
Considerations	• This exercise is an extension of "Selection-Based Imitation" and "Find Same" (Matching mini-manual) • When increasing the distance between index finger and picture, it may be necessary to increase the distance between the pictures.

	Tracking 2 (Direct Point)
Purpose	• To teach the child to track/retrieve objects based on pointing • To teach the child to orient to and track the pointing of others over extended distances. • To teach the child a rudimentary understanding of "this" and "that".
Set up	• Place a few items around the room (on the floor). The objects should be two to three feet apart. You and the child stand in the middle of the room about three feet apart.
Procedure	1. Point to one of the objects and say: "get me that" or "give me this". The child should get the object and give it to you. Initially, it may be helpful if a second person provides manual guidance. When the child hands you the object, provide positive feedback, wait two to three seconds and then present a new direction. 2. Start with close proximity between index finger and target object (10-14 inches) and gradually increase the distance. Eventually, the child should be able to track across the room. 3. Start by standing side by side and point to an object within the child's peripheral vision. As the child catches on, begin pointing to objects outside of the child's visual field. Thus, he will have to orient (move his head and body) in order to track. 4. Once the child can track across the room, vary the position between you and the child i.e. (a) face to face in close proximity, pointing to objects on each side of the child face to face in close proximity, b) pointing to objects behind the child (the child has to turn around to locate the object), (c)

	face to face in close proximity, but you turn around (back to the child) and point to an object in the direction that the child is facing) (d) as described in a, b, and c, but pointing to objects *at a distance* (e) face to face, pointing to objects in front of the child (between you and him) (f) stand behind the child and point as described in a, b, c, d, and e.
Considerations	• Tracking acuity may often require consistent practice over long periods of time. Once the child makes some progress, tracking should be part of most routine interactions. Practice throughout the day as well as during dedicated sessions. • Practice in all environments and all positions. It is important that the child learns to turn their body so to orient toward the target object. • Practice across all distances. When pointing to an object in close proximity, the target object can be closer to other objects. When pointing to an object at a far distance (across the room or outside), the target object should be placed further away from other objects.

	Tracking 3 (Object/Location)
Purpose	• To teach the child to follow directions involving two-part pointing. • To teach the child to shift attention; tracking the attention of instructors when they point to an object and then to a location ("put this over there"). • To teach the child a rudimentary understanding of "this", "that" and "there".
Set up	• Place a few items around the room (on the floor). The room

56

	should be furnished with larger base objects such as chairs, tables, and bins. Stand in the middle of the room with the child.
Procedure	1. Point and say: "put that"- "over there" (point to a location). The child should track to the object, pick it up, and place it the designated location. Initially, a second person may provide manual guidance. 2. When beginning, it may be necessary to separate the two instructions. Thus, delay the second point ("over there") until the child responds to the first ("put that"). With success, gradually decrease the time between the instructions. 3. Use "bounded regions" as the designated location (a chair, an empty table, an empty bin).
Considerations	• This exercise should eventually include persons in addition to locations (i.e., "give that to her/him"). For some children, it may be easier to first acquire this skill using persons rather than locations. • Fluency with two-step object imitation and multi-step instructions could lessen the difficulty of this exercise. • A common problem is that children act on the first instruction ("put this/that") but not the second ("over there"). If the child does not make notable progress within four to five sessions, this exercise should be postponed and revisited upon success with "Tracking 4 (Two Objects)" and/or progress with more advanced receptive language. • When the child demonstrates proficiency with bounded regions ("put this/that over there") and persons ("give that to her/him"), introduce open-ended regions (i.e., point to a general area on the floor). Thus, first point to an object ("put this/that"), then point to a general area on the floor ("over there"). The shift from bounded to open ended

	regions is often difficult and demands extensive practice. However, an understanding of open-ended regions is a fundamental aspect of pragmatic language and cannot be overlooked. • Be mindful that use of "this" and "that" is most often determined by proximity; "this" usually refers to something close-by whereas "that" usually refers farther away. However, this is not an absolute; as with many things in language.

	Tracking 4 (Two Objects)
Purpose	• To teach the child to retrieve two objects based on 'two part pointing' ("get me this and that"/that one and that one") as opposed to placing items following a two-part point ("Tracking 3)
Set up	• Place a few items around the room (on the floor). The items should be approximately the same size and easy to pick up and carry. The objects should be two-three feet apart. You should stand in the middle of the room about three feet from the child.
Procedure	1. Point to one of the objects and say: "get me that", then point to another and say "and...that". The child should bring you both objects. 2. Initially, it may be necessary to separate the two instructions wherein the second instruction is delayed until the child responds to the first. With success, the time between the instructions can be reduced.
Considerations	• Mastery of two-step object imitation and multi- step instruction should assist in success with this exercise.

	• Mastery of this exercise may facilitate "Tracking 3" • Eventually, "give me that and that" should be practiced in conjunction with "put that over there" (placing an object in a location based on two part pointing (see Tracking 3"). If the child demonstrates persistent confusion with this discrimination, these two exercises should be kept separate at this time.

	Tracking 5 (Go to Location)
Purpose	• To teach the child to go to general/open ended regions as directed by a point ("go over there").
Set up	• Stand next to each other in the middle of the room.
Procedure	• Points to a general area on the floor and say; "go there" or "go over there". A second person providing manual guidance makes this exercise easier to execute and should be continued until the child begins to show increased competence.
Considerations	• Proficiencies in "Tracking 3" and "Tracking 4") should lessen difficulties with this exercise. • Many children have a great difficulty understanding the 'concept' of "vicinity" and "regions". This exercise is a cornerstone in development of these concepts and is essential for language and social development.

	Tracking 6 (Combined Tracking and Receptive)
Purpose	• To teach the child to attend to instructions involving both gesture (pointing) and description (receptive)

	• To teach the child that the word "that" in conjunction with pointing aids in the specification of an object (e.g., "that cup" in a field of objects involving other cups).
Set up	• Stand next to each other and have several objects spread across the floor. The child must be able to identify all objects. There should be more than one example of each kind (two kinds of cups, two kinds of balls, etc.). Make sure that pairs of objects are placed close to one another (e.g., two cups are placed next to each other). Thus, when you name an object, children cannot determine which is being referenced unless he considers the instructor's gesture. Likewise, non-matching pairs of objects should be placed close to one another (e.g., a cup and a banana) so when you name an object and point, the child cannot "over select" on the gesture.
Procedure	• Point to an object and say: "Get me that [object name]" (e.g., "get me that cup). The child should track and get the designated object.
Considerations	• The objective of this program is to teach the child to respond to two different cues (modalities) with respect to an object. • The child should be able to identify several objects (Receptive Language mini-manual) and continue to show ease with identifying new ones, and be proficient with basic tracking (see Tracking 1; Tracking 2; Tracking 3.

	Tracking 7 (Alternated Tracking/Receptive)
Purpose	• To teach the child to respond to instructions that combine pointing with a description (e.g., "Put the cup over there")

	• Place a few items around the room (on the floor). The room should be furnished with larger base objects such as chairs, tables, and bins. Stand together in the middle of the room.
Procedure	1. Point to an object and say: "put that one"on the table" (or another familiar location). Do not point to the location. 2. Name an object and point to a location ("put the cup over there"). Do not point to the object.
Considerations	• Many children struggle when pointing and verbal description are combined into one instruction. Initially, it may be necessary to separate the two instructions wherein the second instruction is delayed until the child responds to the first. With success, the interval between instructions can be reduced.

	Shifting Between Instruction Modalities
Purpose	• To strengthen the child's ability to switch flexibly between different kinds of instructions.
Set up	• Place pictures on the wall and corresponding pictures on a table in front of the child; place objects around the room (some objects should correspond to the pictures on the wall). The child is sitting at the table and you are standing by the pictures on the wall.
Procedure	• Present random instructions including: *"Touch same"* (while pointing to a picture on the wall; [see SBI (3) in Matching mini-manual), *"touch this… and this…"* (pointing to two consecutive pictures on the wall: see), *"bring me this…"* (pointing to picture on the wall and the child retrieves the corresponding object,), *"bring me [object name]"* (the child retrieves the object), *"point to [object name]"* (the child

	points to the corresponding picture on the desk), *bring me that* (pointing to object on the floor,), *Bring me this* [object] (pointing to a pair of the same kind of objects,), *put this over there* (pointing to an object and a destination.

Naming and Requesting

	Expressive Naming 1 (Objects)
Purpose	• To teach the child to name objects. • To teach word-object correspondence and ensure that the child is able to name familiar objects in a variety of circumstances and extend the name to similar objects ('basic-level categorization').
Set up	• Sit face to face. Have objects selected for teaching readily available.
Procedure	1. Present an object along with the question, "What is it?" 2. Use conventional discrete trial instruction. 3. Move from mass trials to expanded trials.
Considerations	• Expressive object naming sometimes emerges during receptive object labeling or even at earlier stages of intervention. Some children can already name objects at the onset of intervention. • For some children, it may be better to address receptive identification and expressive naming simultaneously (combined exercises). • For some children, expressive naming is acquired more easily than receptive identification. In such cases, expressive naming may serve as a bridge to teach receptive identification. • Expressive naming is a simple "correspondence skill" (word-object correspondence) and should not be confused with "knowing what an object is". The latter is a much broader

	issue of which expressive naming is merely an element. • Start with familiar objects that are easy for the child to pronounce (e.g., car, ball, cookie, apple). • Start with items that have been acquired receptively (if applicable).
Additional steps and permutations	• As the skill emerges begin including pictures. • When a few items are acquired, merge "Receptive Object Identification. and "Expressive naming 1 (objects). • As soon as the child acquires and retains names with ease, move to less contrived teaching (e.g., see "Tracking and Orienting", "Naming Through Observational Learning".

	Expressive Naming 2 (Body Parts)
Purpose	• Naming *body-parts*
Set up	• Sit face to face.
Procedure	• Point to the one of the child's body parts and ask: "What is it/that?" • Use conventional discrete trial instruction. • Move from mass trials to expanded trials.
Considerations	• If the child struggles with body parts, consider expanding "Expressive Naming 1(Objects)" to increase vocabulary, proficiency, and acquisition speed before reintroducing this exercise. • Some children have significant motor coordination impairments and have great difficulty identifying their own body parts. For children with such difficulties consider an

	increased focus on various eye-hand coordination and gross motor activities.
Additional steps and permutations	• "Expressive body parts" should eventually involve identifying both the child's and the instructor's body parts (See Pronouns mini-manual). Eventually extend to figurines/dolls, animals and pictures.

	Expressive Naming 3 (Persons)
Purpose	• Naming familiar *persons*.
Set up	• Practice with familiar persons (e.g., family members, instructors). As the child learns to name familiar persons, introduce pictures.
Procedure	• Point to a familiar person/picture and ask: "Who is it?" • Use conventional discrete trial instruction. • Move from mass trials to expanded trials.
Considerations	• Some children find it more difficult to name persons than objects and body parts (see Receptive Person Identification", See Early Learning mini-manual). • If the child struggles with Expressive Naming (3), consider expanding "Expressive naming 1 (Objects)" (i.e., increase vocabulary and proficiency) before reintroducing the exercises.

	Expressive Naming: Multiple Presentation Forms
Purpose	• To teach the child to name things with respect to different

	kinds of presentations. In conventional naming protocols, the instructor presents objects one at a time in a discrete fashion. In this exercise, items are presented in other kinds of ways. • To teach the child to 'shift his attention' and to track the attention (point) of another person.

Set up	• *Vary modalities*:
	
	    ○ Present one item at a time (as "Expressive naming 1")
	
	    ○ Point to an object/picture in an array on the table
	
	    ○ Point to a picture in a book
	
	    ○ Point to an object at a distance ("Tracking and Orienting")

Procedure	1. Present the modalities randomly (see "set up") and ask, "What is it?" or "What's this?". 2. If necessary, introduce one modality at a time until child responds flexibly to all modalities
Considerations	• Some children struggle with the transition from contrived conditions ("Expressive naming 1 (objects)" to less constrained natural and varied situations. Expect transition to take time.
Additional steps and permutations	• Use only known objects initially. When the child is proficient, new object names should be taught in all of the ways described. • When pointing, start with short distances (2 feet) and unambiguous arrangements (isolate the target from other objects). Distance and ambiguity can be increased as child makes progress with "Tracking and Orienting" (Tracking and joint attention mini-manual).

	• Use set up as used in Selection Based Imitation (4) but interchange "find this" with "what is this".

	Tracking and orienting
Purpose	• To improve the child's ability to track another person's attention (pointing) • To shift visual orientation to align it with another person • To extend basic naming to less contrived settings. In this exercise, the child names the item to which the instructor points.
Set up	• Place familiar objects and pictures around the room (on a table, wall, floor, shelves, etc.). Instructor and child move around the room.
Procedure	• Point to an object or picture and ask: "What is that?"/What is this?" and while flexibly shifting your attention (and as the child tracks and orients) , also modify the way you ask e.g., "What is this?", "What is that?", "…and what about this?...and this?".
Considerations	• This is an extension of earlier tracking exercises (Tracking and joint attention mini-manual). • Many children struggle when the instructor increases the distance between his finger and the object. When increasing distance, it is often necessary to make the target items more isolated (i.e., increase its distance to surrounding objects).
Additional steps and permutations	• When the child develops proficiency, practice across all settings.

	Sequential Naming
Purpose	• To strengthen *see-say* correspondence and keep track of where the child is in a sequence. • To teach the child to name objects as the child points to them while *moving* about. • To 'detach' naming from antecedent verbal instructions.
Arrangement	• Several familiar objects and/or pictures are placed in a row. The child should stand and face the pictures.
Procedure	1. Point to the table, and say: "What do you see?" or "What are these?" 2. Place yourself behind the child, guide the child's finger (point to the picture farthest to the left) and name each object. When the child imitates your actions, guide the child's finger to the next picture, etc. 3. When the child begins to name items independently, discontinue manual guidance.
Considerations	• This skill may take some time to develop as children often lose track of where they are in the sequence. It may be necessary to build sequential naming gradually, starting with only two items, then three, etc. Initially, it may also be wise spread items out across a large surface so child has to walk from left to right when naming the items. • Sequential naming may establish a foundation for academic skills such as counting and other cognitive skills that require sustained sequential responding (e.g., describing unfolding events, tracking transactions between persons).
Trouble Shooting	• If the child continues to struggle after several instructional segments, it may be wise to postpone the exercise and strengthen/build more proficiency with skills such as "Self-

	Paced Naming" and "Sequential Matching (TPSM)"

	Self-Paced Naming
Purpose	• Increase naming proficiency (the child names known objects at his own pace). • To detach naming from antecedent verbal instruction.
Set up	• Provide the child with a stack of pictures and/or a bin with objects. Use objects/pictures the child can easily name.
Procedure	1. Say: "Name these"/ "What are these?" (Or use similar instructions) and present the materials. The child should select an item, name it, put it away and select the next, etc. 2. Some children have difficulty maintaining a steady pace with the *see-say* correspondence. It may be necessary to start with only a few items and guide the child to name the item only after he places it on the table (i.e., the child selects an item, puts on the table and when he releases, the instructor prompts him to name it).
Considerations	• Self-paced naming may facilitate sequential responding academic skills such as counting. • Self-paced naming will be used as tool skill in order to teach asking "what questions".

	Naming Through Observational Learning
Purpose	• To teach the child new objects names by observing direct instruction with another person.

Set up	• The child observes another person as he learns to name an object (the instructor teaches another person). When the trial ends, the instructor tests to determine if the child learned the name through observation. Use multiple exemplars.
Procedure	1. Present a novel object to another person and say: "This is a [name]", and follow up with the question: "What is it?" The person answers and receives praise. 2. Next, turn to the child, present the object and ask; "What is it?" 3. Repeat the sequence until the child learns the object's name. 4. Continue until the child learns the names of new objects with ease.
Considerations	• Before implementing this exercise, the child should demonstrate success with "Third Person Imitation" and "Follow the Leader" (see Matching mini-manual). • The time delay from observation to test for acquisition should be increased gradually.

	Requesting Desired Objects and Activities
Purpose	• To teach the child to approach someone to request a desired item or activity.
Set up	• When the child is engaged in a preferred activity or is eating a preferred food.
Procedure	1. Arrange so the child is engaged in a preferred activity or eating a preferred food. 2. Block further access to the desired item/activity and instruct

	the child to make a request ("Say, I want X" or "Say, X please").
	3. The child should follow the direction to receive the item.
	4. After 3 to 5 seconds, block access again and wait for the request. If the child does not request, repeat the earlier sequence.
	5. This procedure corresponds to "incidental teaching" and should take place in all settings.
Considerations	• Requesting should be developed from the outset of language intervention and many opportunities should be afforded throughout the day.
	• Practice across all environments.
	• Requesting is not simply the act of uttering a word corresponding to a needed or desired object. It involves approach, directedness (speaking *to* someone), gestures, answering questions, and repairing communication breakdown (i.e., problem solving). Consequently "requesting" is a comprehensive skill that requires many incremental levels of instruction.
	• When teaching the child to request, it is essential to capture or contrive motivation (e.g., capturing desires, arranging tasks where necessary things are missing).
	• Instruction related to requests and "expressive naming" should be addressed concurrently.
	• "Requesting" is often used synonymously with "communication" or "functional communication". This conflation could be misleading. In vernacular parlance "communication" denotes a complex social ability in which a person attempts to make something known to another person. This presupposes that the communicator understands that the other person does not know and must

	be informed. In contrast, requesting can be purely "instrumental" in which another person serves as a tool to fulfill a desire.

	Sequential Matching: Interrupted Chain (TPSM)
Purpose	• To teach the child to request an item required to complete a familiar task.
Set up	• Place four to six pictures face down, in a row on a table. Place a bin containing a set of corresponding items to the child's left (on a separate table or chair). (see "Sequential Matching" in Matching mini-manual). Make sure that one or more of the pertinent objects are not in the bin.
Procedure	1. The child should turn the first picture (T), point to it (P), select the corresponding item from the bin (S), and place it on the picture (M). 2. When the child discovers a picture that lacks a corresponding object, an assistant prompts the child to approach you and request it. 3. Reinstitute the procedure and fade assistance over successive trials.
Considerations	• Prompt fading may take some time. • Intersperse interrupted trials (missing item) with uninterrupted trials (all items available). • This procedure was developed as an alternative to the

[1] Lund, S. K., & Eisenhart, D. E. (2002, May). *Establishing icon-based communication in children with autism and severe cognitive delay.* Poster presented at the *28th Annual Convention for the Association for Behavior Analysis.* Toronto, Canada.

	traditional 'Picture Exchange Communication System' (PECS) as PECS often proves ineffective for highly impaired children[1]. • TPSM works for children who are able to speak. The "Picture Trade" exercise below is designed as an alternative to PECS, specifically for children unable to speak.
Additional steps and permutations	• Once the child requests a missing item reliably, start to address the quality of requesting (eye-contact, volume) and vary the distance child travels. Eventually place yourself out of view so that the child has to look for you.

	Blocked Response (Instruction)
Purpose	• To teach the child to request a needed item in order to carry out an instruction. • To teach the child to ask for information regarding an object's location.
Set up	• Natural environments; known objects. • Two instructors
Procedure	1. Tell the child to get an object ("get the X"). The child should search for the object and bring it to you. Tell the child to get another object. The child should search for the object, but it is hidden). 2. When the child shows signs of giving up the search (stalling, deviates) an assistant guides the child back to you. Model the question: "Where is ___? Or alternatively "I want__" (see "considerations"). 3. You point to the object and say; "there it is" or "it's over there". The child should track and retrieve the object.

Considerations	• The child should be fluent with tracking (see Tracking and joint attention mini-manual) and requesting.
Trouble Shooting	• Many children tend to confuse object requests/demands ("I want __") with "Where is ___?" questions. For some children, this distinction may be too difficult to develop at this stage. If the child does not demonstrate progress, you may settle for object requests ("I want __") and address "Where" questions at a later time. • Most children will be unable to ask questions on demand ("Say...Where is it?") until they are proficient with "Say versus do" (See Verbal imitation.

	Requesting From 2nd Person
Purpose	• To teach the child to request information from a second person when the first person is unable to provide it.
Set up	• Natural environments with known objects. • Two instructors
Procedure	1. Tell the child to get an object ("get the X"). He should search for the object and bring it to you. Then tell him to get another object. He searches for the object, but it is unavailable (i.e., hidden). 2. The child approaches you and asks; "Where is X?" Or alternatively "I want__" (see "considerations" in "Blocked Response"). 3. You say "mommy has it' or "ask mommy". 4. The child should then travel to the designated person, ask for the object and bring it back to you.

Considerations	• The child must be able to ask "Where" questions (see "Blocked response"). • If the child is unable to ask "Where" questions, settle for "I want___" statements and reintroduce "Where" questions at a later time (see "Blocked Response"), for considerations) • This exercise is highly complex and demands that the child make several pragmatic decisions. For greater scaffolding, use "Sequential Matching: Interrupted Chain" as the antecedent condition. • For relevant commentary see Lovaas 1977 pp. 77, 163 ('Giving and seeking information').
Additional steps and Permutations	• As the child shows proficiency, require they "search" for the second person. If they have difficulty locating the second person, prompt them to ask, "Where is (person)?

	Managing Listener's Responses
Purpose	• To teach the child to respond to a variety of situations when requesting an object. • To teach problem solving.
Set up	• Interrupted chains and natural environments. • Two instructors.
Procedure	• When the child requests a missing item (e.g., in the context of an interrupted chain) you may: 1. Provide the requested item (the child says "thank you") 2. Ask: "Do you want this?" (Present an item) (The child says "yes" or "no" accordingly) (See, Yes No Negation in ABA

	Mini-manual: Level Two).
	3. Point to location and say, "It's over there" (see Tracking and joint attention mini-manual).
	4. Present two objects of the kind requested (i.e., two different cups), and ask: "Which one?" (The child should point to one of the items and say "this one").
	5. Tell the child where it is ("It is in the drawer" see Receptive language mini-book).
	6. Tell the child to ask someone else (i.e., "Daddy has it") (see "Requesting from Second Person").
Considerations	• Some of the above situations require separate exercises/isolated practice. For instance, answering yes/no may need to be taught in a different setting before incorporating it in this exercise.
Additional steps and permutations	• Additional obstacles could eventually be added to this routine. For example, if the child is directed to an item on a top shelf, he might then need to request help to get it down.

	Naming to Requesting (contrived)
Purpose	• To 'connect' naming and requesting so that when learning a name of an object there is a direct transfer to requesting. Thus, if the child has learned to name objects through direct instruction, the child should be able to request them under appropriate conditions without explicit teaching.
Set up	• "Sequential Matching: Interrupted Chain and novel items (pictures and objects).
Procedure	1. Teach the child to name a novel item (target) using direct instruction.

	2. Implement "Sequential Matching: Interrupted Chain where the target is missing.
	3. The child requests the missing item.
	4. If the child is unable to request the missing item (i.e., forgot the name), discontinue the segment and practice expressive naming 1.
	5. Return to step 2.
Considerations	• This exercise takes considerable time to run and may require many repetitions. • Bridging naming and requesting is imperative in order to move to advanced language exercises. • This exercise may be implemented when the child begins to identify and name things with relative ease. Occasionally, the exercise can be implemented successfully from the very outset of language intervention.

	Requesting to Naming
Purpose	• To connect requesting and naming so that learning the former transfers directly to the latter. Thus, if a child learns to request an object through direct instruction, he will be able to name the object without explicit teaching.
Set up	• "Sequential Matching: Interrupted Chain and novel items (pictures and objects).
Procedure	• Arrange "Sequential Matching: Interrupted Chain" where novel items are missing. When the child approaches you to request the missing item, prompt correct response (provide the name in the prompted request), deliver the item, and reintroduce "Sequential Matching: Interrupted Chain". If the

	child requests the target item independently on this second trial, afford him a short break, then ask him to name the object ("What is it?").
Considerations	• This exercise demands considerable memory since the time delay between prompting (time of request) and new response opportunity is often a matter of minutes. Extensive practice may be necessary.
Troubleshooting	• A number of things could happen when a child approaches an instructor to request the novel item; (a) the child may stall (since he has no name for the missing item), (b) he may point to the picture of the novel item, (c) he may invent a name for the missing item (e.g., use a name of an object with similar physical features), (d) discontinue the task (give up), or (e) cry or tantrum. In all cases, prompt the correct response and ensure that the child completes the task.

	Receptive-Expressive Correspondence
Purpose	• To connect receptive identification and naming so that learning one modality yields the other. Thus, if you teach the child to identify an object receptively, he will be able to name it without direct instruction.
Set up	• The child and instructor sit at a table containing a few familiar items and one novel item.
Procedure	• Teach the child to identify the novel item receptively or name it. Once he learns an item in one modality (e.g., receptive), test for the other modality (expressive) Example 1: Teach "eraser" receptively, then probe naming when he discriminates it from other known objects.

78

	Example 2: Teach "tissue" expressively, then when he remembers the name in expanded trials, probe receptive identification.
Considerations	• Bridging these modalities is imperative in order to move towards more advance language exercises. • Typically, it is easier for children to go from expressive to receptive than the other way around.
Additional steps and permutations	• Gradually increase the time between the teaching trial and test trial. • Receptive-expressive correspondence exercises can be arranged in different ways that would also include natural settings. For instance, tell the child to bring an item for which they have not yet learned the name. Point to the item and tell the child to get it (using the name). When the child returns, follow-up with asking child "What's this?).

	Receptive to Requesting
Purpose	• To connect receptive identification and requesting so that learning one modality yields the other. Thus, if you teach the child to identify an object receptively, he will be able to request this item without direct instruction.
Set up	• "Sequential Matching: Interrupted Chain" and novel items (pictures and objects).
Procedure	1. Teach the child to identify a novel item receptively. 2. Implement "Sequential Matching: Interrupted Chain" where the target item is missing. 3. If the child is unable to request the missing item (i.e., forgot the name), discontinue this segment and practice receptive

	identification (step 1). 4. Return to step 2.
Considerations	• In order to implement this exercise successfully, the child should show some progress with "Receptive-Expressive Correspondence".

	Matching, Receptive and Naming
Purpose	• To teach the child to shift flexibly between different instructions and modalities. The child will learn to shift between instructions such as "Do this" while pointing to a picture ("Selection-Based Imitation"), "find one of these"/find this one" (searching), "What is this?" ("Naming"), and "Point to the _x_" ("Receptive Identification").
Set up	• The child is at a desk about six-seven feet away from the wall (or a large board). Place an array of known pictures on the desk and attach corresponding (and non-corresponding) pictures to the wall; place objects corresponding to the instructor's pictures around the floor.
Procedure	• Present one of the following instructions: "Do this"/ "find this one" (while pointing to a picture on the wall)"; "What is it? (pointing to a picture on the wall); "point to the ___" [one of the child's pictures]; "bring me a __[referring to one of the objects on the floor]. An assistant prompts from behind.
Considerations	• Shifting flexibly between different instructions may be challenging to some children. Difficulties may be compounded if the child has been exposed to extensive "compartmental teaching" (i.e., one kind of 'program' at a

	time).

	Picture Swap
Purpose	• To teach children to exchange pictures for items they desire. (For children who are not able to vocalize requests).
Set up	• In front of the child place an array of pictures and an array of items represented in the pictures. The two rows are arranged so the *pictures correspond in terms of position*. The rows may be arranged so both are oriented toward the child. **(See Fig. 6).** • One of the items (and its picture match) is a highly preferred item. • It's best to have a third person to assist with the prompting. Prompt from standing behind the child.
Procedure	• Step one: As the child reaches for the preferred item (you've completed a reinforcer survey), the assistant prompts the child, before they are able to get it, to pick up the corresponding picture and guide the child to hand that picture to you. Immediately, provide the child the item in exchange for the item. • Step two: Change the positions of the items so that they no longer correspond by position. **(See Fig. 7)** repeat the procedure as in step one. • Step three: When you see the child begin to reach for the picture fade the presence of the actual items so that only pictures are available. • Step four: Increase the number of preferred items and distractors.

81

	• Begin to systematically increase the distance between the child (who is in possession or in close proximity to the pictures) and the adult.
Considerations	• This approach immediately cements the relationship between the actual item and its representation by insisting the child make a conditional discrimination.
	• It's not always necessary that children have demonstrated 2d-3d matching abilities. Sometimes this program serves to strengthen those relationships without first running traditional matching programs because of the built in reinforcement.
	• It is important to keep in mind that if children learn to make the discrimination, they have not learned the name of the item they have selected. It is still important to teach the names of the item the child selects using receptive identification protocols above. This will be important later when teaching "yes"/"no" to desired objects (see ABA Mini-manual" Yes-No-Negation.
	• This initial step contrasts with PECs protocols. In PECS, the first step requires only one picture on the table; thus, children are not required to attend to what it is a picture of. Consequently, children often learn only to 'pick up and deliver whatever is in front' of them without regard for correspondence. This often, in our experience, interferes with the later requirement to make a conditional discrimination.
	• It is important for many children that the representation be as close to the actual item as possible. Therefore, we use pictures, not drawings (at least in the very beginning of training) and absolutely not symbols.
	• If after the actual items are faded, the child selects pictures, which do not correspond to reinforcers, it may be necessary to strengthen matching abilities, particularly 2d-3d and 3d-

	2d.

Figure 6

Figure 7

Categorization

	Category Match - Receptive Follow-up
Purpose	• To teach the child to match items by category.
Set up	• Place at least two samples from three different categories (e.g., food, vehicles, clothing) on separate plates or in separate bins.
Procedure	*Step one* Hand the child a different picture of a member of one of categories present on the table and say "Put with (category). Use hand over hand prompt and gradually fade prompts. *Step two*: Receptive follow-up; Ask the child to 'touch or find' (category) after matching correctly. Thus say, "match vehicles" > child matches > say, "Find vehicles > child identifies vehicles. For many children this helps to establish the category name. Make sure to intersperse trials so that the request to 'find' is not always followed immediately after matching.
Considerations	• Expand to other pertinent categories. • Category 'sorting' [(use the same protocols from Matching-sorting exercises (1 and 2)] should be considered if a child struggles with identification of categories when using 'receptive follow-up'.

	Receptive Categorization: **Proper Name vs Category name**

Purpose	• To teach the child to assign higher-order descriptions (category names). • To teach the child to accept that a single object can be referred to by its proper name (basic-level) and a category name (super-ordinate level); that each object has a unique name (cookie) as well as a name shared by other objects with similar function (food).
Set up	• Objects the child can name. Start with two distinct and salient categories (e.g., food and clothing). • Display one object of each kind on the table.
Procedure	• Select two different kinds of objects (e.g., cookie and shoe) Vary the instructions: "Point to the [object name]" and "point to the [category name].
Considerations	• Expand to other pertinent categories (e.g., furniture, food, animals). • Categorization sits under early verbal reasoning abilities comparing and contrasting. The same item belongs to multiple categories across different dimensions; e.g., parts, color, size, location, function, material, property, etc. (ABA Mini-Manual eBooks cover some of these.)

	Naming Categories 1
Purpose	• To teach the child to assign higher-order description (category names) to objects. • To teach the child when to use basic description and when to use higher order description.
Set up	• "Category containers" with three or more items of the same category. For instance: Animals (dog, sheep, cow) clothing

	(hat, shoe, mitten) and food (cookie, pizza, hot dog).
Procedure	• *Step 1*: Three 'category' containers with three or more examples in each. Point to a container and ask: "What is in here?" Prompt the child to say the category name (e.g., "animals"). Point to the next container, etc. Vary the items and position of the containers. Teach to proficiency. • *Step 2*: Three containers with three or more examples in two of them and a single item on one of them. For instance: Animals (dog, sheep, cow) clothing (hat) and food (cookie, pizza, hot dog). Point to a container and ask: "What is in here?" If the container has several objects (dog, sheep, cow), prompt the child to say the category name ("animals"). If the container has one single item (cookie), prompt the child to name the item ("cookie"). Point to the next container, etc. Vary the items and position of the containers. Alternate 'single item containers' and "category containers". For instance, if *cookie* was the single item container in one trial, it should be in a category container in the next (cookie, pizza, hot dog). Vice versa, a 'category container' in one trial (e.g., "animals") should be dismantled in the next ('dog'). • *Step 3:* Three 'category' containers with three or more examples in each. Point to a container and ask: "What is in here?" The child says the category name (e.g., "animals"). Pick up a single item from one of the containers (this may include the container he just named) and ask the child: "What is this?" Prompt the child to say the proper name (e.g., "dog"). Point to the next container, etc. Alternate questions about category containers and single objects.
Considerations	• If the child struggles with this strategy, it may be necessary to begin by using standard approaches (See Leaf and McEachin, 1999 p. 241).

	Naming Categories 2
Purpose	• To teach the child to assign higher-order description (category names) to objects. • To teach the child when to use basic description and when to use higher order description.
Set up	• Three 'category' containers with one example in each. Place several 'category items' on the table outside of the bin.
Procedure	• *Exercise 1*: Point to on object on the table and ask: "What is it". When the child names it, instruct him to "put it with the same" (or "Where does it go?") and prompt him to place it in the right 'category container'. Continue to fill up the containers. When a 'category container' has more than one item, you may alternate the instructions "put with the same" and "put with the [category name]" (e.g., "put with the food"). • *Exercise 2*: Ask the child to identify an object on the table. When the child does, instruct the child to "put it with the same" (or "Where does it go?") and prompt the child to place it in the right 'category container'. Continue to fill up the containers. When the child is proficient, intersperse with questions from Naming Categories (1) steps 2 and 3.
Considerations	• Once the child has mastered these expressive category exercises, children should learn to relate things within and across categories (see ABA Mini eBook: Same-different).

	Reciprocal Categories
Purpose	• To teach the child to alternate appropriately between higher-order naming (category naming) and basic level

	naming
Set up	• Sit face to face; you both have access to a pile of common objects. An assistant sits behind the child.
Procedure	• *Step 1*: Pick two objects of the same category from the pile (e.g. cracker and a piece of cheese), hold them up and say: "I have food". The second instructor, guides child to select two objects of a different category (e.g. a dog and a bear), hold it up and reciprocate by using the appropriate category name ("I have animals"). • *Step 2:* Pick two items from different categories and say ("I have [object name] and [object name]"). The child reciprocates by picking two items from different categories and say "I have [object name] and [object name]". The instructor then puts the items down and picks two items from the same category (e.g., cracker and a piece of cheese), holds them up and say: "I have some food". The assistant, guides child to select two objects of a different category (e.g., a dog and a bear), hold them up and reciprocate by using the appropriate category name ("I have some animals"). Alternate between these two conditions until the child discovers the language game.
Additional steps and permutations	• This extension involves two new components (1) the child must discern when to reciprocate one versus two statements (i.e., differentiate the instructor's behavior), and (2) appropriate use of the conjunction "and". This exercise should also be done in situations when the two objects are the same (e.g., spoons). Thus, child will have to discern when to use a conjunction or the plural (e.g., "I have cup**s**" versus "I have cup and doll").

	Describing kinds
Purpose	• To learn the meaning of "kind".
Set up	• Place several objects from different categories on a table in front of the child.
Procedure	• Step 1: Ask: "What kind of animal do you have?"/ "What kind of food do you have?", etc. Prompt the child to apply the appropriate category name. • Step 2: Same as step one, but ask additional relevant questions such as "where is it?" and "What color is it?" Thus, when the child answers "What kind of [category name] do you have? Follow up with "Where is it? (The child points and says "here") and/or "What color is it?", etc.)

REFERENCES

Leaf, R., & McEachin, J. (1999). *A work in progress: Behavior management strategies and a curriculum for intensive behavioral treatment of autism.* New York: DRL Books.

Lovaas, O.I. (1977). *The autistic child: Language development through behavior modification.* New York: Irvington Publishers, Inc.

Lund, S. K. (2004). Selection-based imitation: A tool skill in the development of receptive language in children with autism. *The Behavior Analyst Today, Vol. 5, No 1,* 27-36.

Lund, S. K., & Eisenhart, D. (2002, May). Establishing icon-based communication in children with autism and severe cognitive delay. Poster presented at the *28th Annual Convention of the Association for Behavior Analysis,* Toronto, Canada.

About the Author

Dr. Schnee is a recognized expert in early intensive, ABA-based, language-focused, intervention. He earned a Ph.D. in clinical psychology from Georgia State University and is board certified in applied behavior analysis. Dr. Schnee has 30+ years of experience designing and supervising early intensive behavioral intervention programs; domestically and internationally. He is the founder and former director or Nexus Language Builders, an ABA, center-based program that offered full day, 1:1 intervention to children on the spectrum. He now provides concierge consultation services to families locally (in the New York metropolitan area, nationally and internationally. For more information about Dr. Schnee, go to www.nexusais.com .

Additional Publications:

Paperback versions of this book and the *Mini-Manual; Level Two* are available on Amazon.

https://www.amazon.com/ABA-Mini-Manual-Imitation-
Receptive/dp/B0BTNSKK1H/ref=sr_1_3?crid=3FXZBKOSI2HS6&keywords=alan%20schne
e%20books&qid=1680624598&sprefix=alan%20schnee%2Caps%2C107&sr=8-
3&fbclid=IwAR2a7-UwWQDkMWTnR4HfzXBHmHkmv_-
jn1o9RIPP_hmx_WOL4BW1FyfkZvM

Kindle mini-manuals

17 separate kindle mini-manuals for each of 17 domains contained in Levels One and Two are
available on Amazon USA and many other countries.

https://www.amazon.com/gp/product/B0BT8PPP1J?ref_=dbs_p_mng_rwt_ser_shvlr&stor
eType=ebooks

Made in the USA
Las Vegas, NV
13 October 2023